NEW VANGUARD • 151

KRIEGSMARINE COASTAL FORCES

GORDON WILLIAMSON   ILLUSTRATED BY IAN PALMER

First published in Great Britain in 2008 by Osprey Publishing,
PO Box 883, Oxford, OX1 9PL, UK
PO Box 3985, New York, NY 10185-3985, USA
Email: info@ospreypublishing.com

Osprey Publishing is part of the Osprey Group.

Transferred to digital print on demand 2014.

First published 2008
2nd impression 2009

Printed and bound by Cadmus Communications, USA.

A CIP catalogue record for this book is available from the British Library.

ISBN: 978 1 84603 331 5
PDF e-book ISBN: 978 1 84603 820 4

Page layout by Melissa Orrom Swan, Oxford
Index by Margaret Vaudrey
Typeset in Sabon and Myriad Pro
Originated by PDQ Digital Media Solutions Ltd.

The Woodland Trust
Osprey Publishing are supporting the Woodland Trust, the UK's leading woodland
conservation charity, by funding the dedication of trees.

www.ospreypublishing.com

CONTENTS

KRIEGSMARINE COASTAL FORCES

INTRODUCTION

Understandably, when studying the surface fleets of most of the world's navies the readers' imagination is most readily captured by the capital ships such as aircraft carriers and battleships; due to their visual impression of massive strength, service in such vessels has always had an aura of glamour. This is shared by the much smaller but equally deadly submarines, whose dramatic operations have the added appeal of the intimacy of a small crew, in which we may find ourselves identifying with individuals.

However, the capital warships – being extremely costly, not just in cash terms but also in material, industrial and manpower resources – inevitably formed only a small proportion of any navy's total order of battle. In terms of ship numbers and manhours, the great bulk of the hard daily sea-duty was to be found in the smaller, decidedly unglamorous world of support vessels. Without these ships no fleet could function, and the World War II Kriegsmarine was no exception. Germany's minesweepers alone formed a massive proportion of its total strength, and are very much the unsung heroes of the Kriegsmarine. Very little has been written of their wartime service, despite a significant number of their personnel being highly decorated. The award rolls of the German Cross in Gold, the Knight's Cross of the Iron Cross and the Roll of Honour of the German Navy all contain the names of several members of the coastal forces, whose war was equally, if not more hazardous than that of comrades serving in branches better known to the public. In fact, many of these officers and seamen continued to carry out dangerous duties well after the war ended, clearing mines from around coastal waters under British supervision in the GMSA (German Mine Sweeping Administration).

Apart from essential minesweeping and minelaying tasks, smaller branches of the Kriegsmarine were responsible for escort duties, patrol services, fleet auxiliary roles such as refuelling, hospital and accommodation ships and sail training. The vast number of variants that existed (to say nothing of the wide range of captured enemy vessels pressed into service in such roles) precludes detailed coverage here of every type of ship; this work therefore concentrates on the main types, those that performed the bulk of the Navy's work, predominantly in coastal or home waters.

FAR LEFT
The War Badge for Minesweepers, etc. It is an interesting departure from normal war badge designs in showing an action (the waterspout from an underwater explosion) rather than illustrating a specific type of vessel. This was perfectly logical, considering the wide range of vessels and duties associated with the Sicherungsverbände. (Author's collection)

LEFT
The award document for the Minesweeper badge, one of many variants that were produced. This document was issued to Bootsmannsmaat Karl Heesemann, a rating who went on to become a commissioned officer. Many sailors spent time on minesweepers before going on to serve in other branches of the surface fleet. (Author's collection)

THE SECURITY BRANCH

In the simplest terms, the Navy under the Naval High Command (Oberkommando der Kriegsmarine) was split into three main operational commands: the Flottenchef, covering the major combat units of the Fleet, and the Kommandierender Admiral der Marinestationen der Nordsee and der Ostsee, the Commanding Admirals of the North Sea and Baltic Naval Stations.

Under these latter two senior commands came the Befehlshaber der Sicherung der Nordsee and der Ostsee, Commanders of Security in the North Sea and Baltic.

On the outbreak of war in September 1939 the position of Befehlshaber der Sicherung was held by a flag officer with the rank of Konteradmiral. As more and more territory, and thus coastal waters, fell under German control, so new senior naval commands were established (e.g. in Paris, Oslo, Sofia, etc), and each had a number of units of the Sicherungsverbände under its control. In November 1944, as German-controlled waters rapidly shrank, Sicherungsverbände units were grouped under the command of the Befehlshaber der Sicherungstreitkräfte or Commander of Security Forces. Below these senior levels in the chain of command came the positions of Führer der Minensuchboote and Führer der Vorpostenboote, Commanders of Minesweepers and of Patrol Boats.

For the greater part of the war those naval units (usually of flotilla size) responsible for minesweeping, minelaying, patrol and escort work were grouped into Security Divisions or Sicherungsdivisionen – of which 11 were ultimately created, plus one training unit, the Sicherungslehrdivision. For example, in 1941, I. Sicherungsdivision comprised the following units:

15. Minensuchflottille
22. Minensuchflottille
32. Minensuchflottille
34. Minensuchflottille
13. Vorpostenflottille

OPPOSITE
A young Fähnrich (midshipman) in dress uniform, with dagger and *portepee*. His rank is indicated by his narrow shouldercords, and the lack of cuff rings below the star of the seaman's branch on his sleeve. His combat experience is evidenced by the ribbon of the Iron Cross 2nd Class worn in the buttonhole; on his left breast, in the regulation position, he proudly displays the War Badge for Minesweepers, Sub-Chasers and other units of the Sicherungsverbände. (Deutsches U-Boot-Museum)

A trio of minesweepers – 66, 98 & 145 – tied up in port before the war. Although they are finished in the old black colour scheme, under magnification one can still see the large bronze eagle-and-swastika mounted on the front of the bridges of 98 and 145. This dates the photo to 1935 at the earliest, when the Reichsmarine was re-formed as the Kriegsmarine. (Author's collection)

20. Vorpostenflottille

Minenräumschiff 12

Sperrbrecher 145, 147, 148 & 149

As early as 1940, a special badge was introduced to recognize the service of personnel involved in such essential duties. Designed by the respected Berlin graphic artist Otto Placzek, it was authorized on 31 August 1940 by Grossadmiral Raeder, and entitled the Kriegsabzeichen für Minensuch-, U-Bootsjagd- und Sicherungsverbände (War Badge for Minesweeper, Sub-Chaser and Security Units). Awards began on 11 September of that year, the badge being available to those who had completed a minimum of three combat missions. Like the other War Badges of the armed services, this was issued together with an award document; it was recorded in the individual's pay book and service records, and was worn on the left breast of uniforms.

The metal badge consisted of a vertical oval wreath of oakleaves topped by the eagle with a tiny swastika in its talons. In the centre of the wreath was a waterspout rising from the sea, which could indicate either a detonating mine in the mine-clearing role, or a detonating depth charge in the sub-chaser role. The wreath and eagle were gilded, surrounding a silvered waterspout on a toned silver sea. The reverse featured either a vertical or horizontal hinged pin fitting.

The badge was re-authorized in 1957 with the eagle and swastika removed, for wear by veterans or those still serving in the Bundesmarine.

MINESWEEPERS (Minensuchboote)

At the time the Kriegsmarine was formed in 1935 many of its existing minesweepers were rather elderly veterans of the Great War. The first modern class to be introduced was the Minensuchboot M35. This proved to be a successful and highly seaworthy vessel with a relatively powerful armament for vessels of this category. It was, however, of fairly complex construction and expensive to produce. The powerplant required extensive and careful maintenance by skilled technicians, a situation that may have been acceptable in peacetime but was less so after wartime manpower demands put great pressure on the numbers of such skilled personnel available. During the latter part of the war the fact that these vessels had oil-fired boilers also restricted their use due to fuel shortages.

Minesweepers were not named, but were given a pennant number prefixed with the letter 'M'.

Minensuchboot M35

The M35 was constructed by a number of different shipyards, and a total of 68 were built. Of this number just over 30 were lost in action during the war. Those that survived were distributed amongst the Allies, with 17 given to the US Navy, 13 to the Soviets, and 5 to the Royal Navy. The US Navy returned five of its M35s to the new German Bundesmarine in the mid 1950s. Production was as follows:

Shipyard	Vessels	Total
Stülken, Hamburg	M1–3, 10, 13–16, 25–28	12
Oderwerke, Stettin	M4–6, 11, 17–19, 29–32, 151–156	17
Flenderwerke, Lübeck	M7–9, 12, 20–24	9
Lübecker Maschinenbaugesellschaft, Lübeck	M33–34, 81–85	7
Schichau, Elbing	M35–36	2
Atlas Werke, Bremen	M37–39	3
Rickmerswerft, Wesermünde	M101–104	4
Lindenau, Memel	M131–132	2
AG Neptun, Rostock	M201–206	6
Deutsche Werft, Hamburg	M251–256	6

Specifications:			
Length	68m	Powerplant	2x Lentz 3200hp expansion engines
Beam	8.7m	Top speed	18 knots
Displacement	870 tons	Endurance	5,000 nautical miles
Armament	2x 10.5cm gun, 1x 3.7cm flak, 2x 2cm flak; 4x depth charge launchers; up to 30 mines	Crew	107

As the war progressed, the need to beef up the anti-aircraft armament on most Kriegsmarine vessels led to the M35 minesweepers having the single 2cm flak mount either side of the bridge replaced with twin mounts, and in some cases the aft single flak mount was replaced with a quadruple 2cm Flakvierling. Light machine guns could also be fitted.

Minensuchboot M40

This type was of similar specification to the M35 but utilized a simpler method of construction, and featured coal-fired rather than oil-fired boilers, making them less dependent on Germany's dwindling oil reserves in the second half of the war. A total of 131 of the class were built, predominantly in shipyards in occupied Holland. These boats did not replace the M35 class, production of which continued. Around half of the M40 boats built were lost in action during the war; of those that survived 25 went to the US Navy, 30 to the Soviets and 13 to the Royal Navy. As with the M35s, five of the boats that had served in the US Navy were returned to the new Bundesmarine in the 1950s. (Interestingly, a handful of this highly successful type were still serving in the Romanian Navy in the mid 1990s.) Production numbers in the various yards were are shown on p.10.

Sailors under training on the forward 10.5cm gun of a minesweeper. Later versions had a protective turret; manning an exposed gun like this in heavy weather must have been quite an experience. (Author's collection)

RIGHT
A flotilla of minesweepers on operations; the flag bearing the Iron Cross on a horizontal tricolour dates this photo between 1933 and November 1935. These older coal-burning vessels would be the first ship to which many Kriegsmarine sailors would be posted. As wartime oil fuel shortages began to bite, the older coal-burning ships proved valuable once again. (Author's collection)

BELOW, RIGHT
An M35 type minesweeper, backbone of the Kriegsmarine's minesweeper fleet. The wartime censor has made a half-hearted effort to disguise the vessel's pennant number '1', still just visible below the forward 10.5cm gun turret. (Author's collection)

As with the M35 type, these boats were eventually up-gunned, the ultimate version carrying one 10.5cm gun, two twin and one single 3.7cm flak, one 2cm Flakvierling, two twin 2cm flak and two machine guns.

MINESWEEPERS

1: Early pre-war type

This is one of the minesweepers used by the Reichsmarine, built in about 1919. A number of these vessels continued in service during (and even briefly after) World War II. The usual colour scheme for these coal-burning vessels until 1936–37 was black, as shown. Typical features are the tall narrow funnel and the exposed main armament; enclosed turrets were only added on later models.

2: M35 class

The M35 type was the mainstay of the Kriegsmarine's minesweeper force in World War II. Note the main armament of two 10.5cm guns, now in enclosed turrets. With an additional single 3.7cm and four 2cm anti-aircraft guns, these vessels were much more heavily armed than their predecessors. The plan view shows the rails running along the after deck, along which mines were rolled and dropped over the stern.

(Detail, left) An essential part of the equipment inventory of any minesweeper was the paravane, resembling a tiny aircraft or winged bomb. These were towed on cables either side of the vessel, their vanes being set to steer them away from the hull on each side to form an arrowhead-shaped swept area. They would snag the anchor cables of enemy mines, which slid down the tow cables into a cutting mechanism on the paravane. Once the mine had bobbed to the surface it could be detonated from a safe distance by gunfire.

(Detail, right) The standard German EMC mine of World War II was attached by a cable to a small trolley which also acted as its anchor. Once it was dropped from the minelayer the cable would unreel, allowing the mine to rise to just below the surface.

1: Early pre-war type

2: M35 class

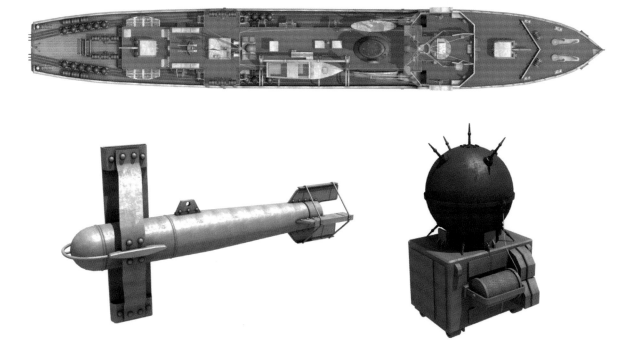

Shipyard	Vessels	Total
Atlas Werke, Bremen	M261–267	7
Rickmerswerft, Wesermünde	M271–279	9
Lindenau, Memel	M291–294	4
Unterweser Schiffsbaugesellschaft, Lehe	M301–307	7
Oderwerke, Stettin	–	8
Lübecker Maschinenbaugesellschaft, Lübeck	M329–330	2
AG Neptun, Rostock	M341–348	8
Schichau, Elbing	M361–377	17
Elsflether Werft, Elsflether	M381–389	9
Rotterdamsche Doorgdok Maatschappij, Rotterdam	M401–408	8
N.V. Koninklijke Maatschappij De Schelde, Vlissingen	M411–416	6
N.V. Dok en Werf Maatschappij Wilton-Feijenoord, Schiedam	M421–428	8
N.V. Nederlandsche Scheepsbouw Maatschappij, Amsterdam	M431–438	8
N.V. Burghout's Machinefabriek & Scheepswerf, Amsterdam	M441–446	6
N.V. Werf Gusto, Schiedam	M451–456	6
Nederlandsche Dok Maatschappij, Amsterdam	M459–463	5
Scheepswerf Van der Giessen & Zonen, Krimpen aan den Lek	M467–471	5
J & K Smit, Kinderdijk	M475–476	2
Boele's Scheepswerven & Machinefabriek, Bolnes	M483–484	2
Scheepswerf en machinefabriek Verschure & Co, Amsterdam	M486	1
N.V. L. Smit & Zoon's Scheeps- en Werktuigbouw, Kinderdijk	M489	1
N.V. Scheepsbouwwerf Gebr. Pot, Bolnes	M495–496	2

Specifications:

Length	62.3m	Powerplant	2x 2400hp expansion engines
Beam	8.9m	Top speed	17 knots
Displacement	775 tons	Endurance	4,000 nautical miles
Armament	1x 10.5cm gun, 1x 3.7cm flak, 2x 2cm flak; 4x depth charge launchers; up to 30 mines	Crew	74

This port-side view of an M35 class minesweeper shows the distinctive so-called 'goalpost' davit for the ship's launch. Note also the raised flaps on the forward turret, unmasking the optics for the main gun. This vessel is Minesweeper M19, serving with 3. Minensuchflottille. (Author's collection)

Minensuchboot M43

This final minesweeper type to be built for the Kriegsmarine made use of prefabricated sections, so construction could be dispersed and only final assembly required shipyard facilities. Although more than 160 were ordered only 17 were ultimately built, though a number of others were in various stages of completion when the war ended. Far more powerfully armed and, like the M40s, equipped with coal-fired boilers, examples of these vessels served on into the 1960s. Completed production was as follows:

Shipyard	Vessels	Total
AG Neptun, Rostock	M601–612	12
Schichau, Königsberg	M801–805	5

Specifications:				
Length	67.8m	Powerplant	2x 2400hp expansion engines
Beam	9m	Top speed	17 knots
Displacement	821 tons	Endurance	3,600 nautical miles
Armament	2x 10.5cm guns, 2x 3.7cm flak, 1x 2cm Flakvierling; 4x depth charge launchers; up to 24 mines	Crew	90

A trio of minesweepers at sea. As well as carrying out basic mine clearing (and minelaying) operations, minesweepers were also used to escort small coastal convoys and for anti-submarine work. Note the liferaft attached to the bridge of the nearest ship. (Author's collection)

Operational deployment

The ubiquitous M35 minesweeper served on virtually every front on which the Kriegsmarine was involved, from the Arctic to the Mediterranean. The 42 minesweeper flotillas were based as follows; note that 'Channel' means 'English Channel', and active dates which conclude after 1945 refer to units that were maintained post-war for mine clearing under Allied control:

Any coastal vessels operating in Western waters ran the risk of attack by British aircraft. Judging from the victory tally on the bridge, this crew considered themselves more than capable of putting up a robust defence. Under magnification nine plane silhouettes can be made out, all dated 1941 and 1942; six are in solid black, three in outline only, and the two at the tips of the arc-shaped display are specifically shown as twin-engined types. In the centre of the arc is the faint white outline of what may be an MGB. (Author's collection)

B | M35 MINESWEEPER

This sectional view shows a typical minesweeper of this class. These small warships were designed for use in coastal waters, and, compared to larger vessels, they spent limited time at sea on any one cruise, so they were provided with little in the way of accommodation. The forward part of the hull, under the forward gun turret, contained the junior ratings' accommodation, with the petty officers' quarters immediately below. The lowest deck in this area housed the ship's stores and the magazine for the forward turret.

Midships were the No.1 and No.2 boiler rooms, venting into a single funnel. Immediately aft of the boiler rooms was the electrical generator, with the ship's galley above it.

Further aft is the engine room, with two Lentz steam turbines driving twin screws. In the lowest level aft of the engine room were further stores compartments, another electrical generator room, and the magazine for the aft turret. Immediately above this was the accommodation for officers and senior ranks.

Just aft of the stern turret the paravanes can be seen lashed to the railings. Also visible towards the aft end of the deck are a number of mines on their wheeled trolleys, ready to be dropped over the stern.

Just forward of the stern 2cm Flakvierling gun is a 1m optical rangefinder for this weapon; the 3m rangefinder which controlled the main armament is mounted on the bridge.

Slung from 'goalpost' davits on the starboard side just aft of the funnel is a large motor pinnace, and a small jollyboat is carried on the port side. In addition one or more small liferafts were carried, often mounted on the sides of the forward turret or on the face of the bridge.

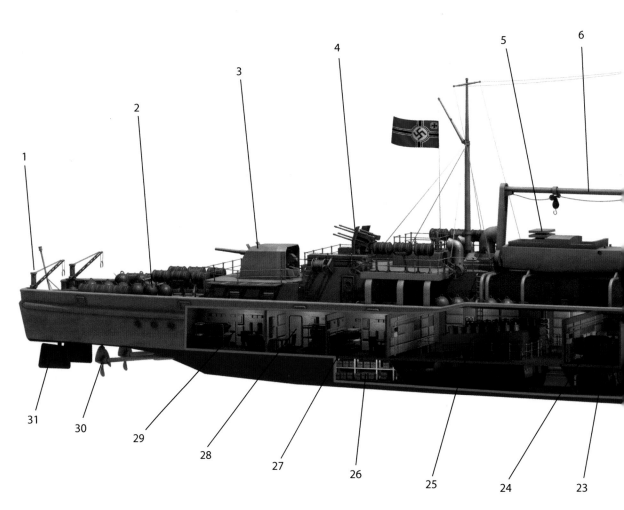

KEY

1 Stern derricks
2 Mines
3 Aft 10.5cm turret
4 2cm Flakvierling
5 Ship's launch
6 Launch gantry
7 Ship's boat
8 Funnel
9 Crows Nest
10 Searchlight
11 Main armament rangefinder

12 Bridge
13 Forward 10.5cm turret
14 Bosun's Room
15 Office
16 Mess
17 Magazine
18 Junior NCO accommodation
19 Ship's stores
20 Crew accommodation
21 Boiler No. 2
22 Boiler No. 1

23 Stabiliser compartment
24 Electrical generator room
25 Engine room
26 Ship's stores
27 Senior NCO accommodation
28 Senior NCO accommodation
29 Officer accommodation
30 Twin propellers
31 Twin rudders

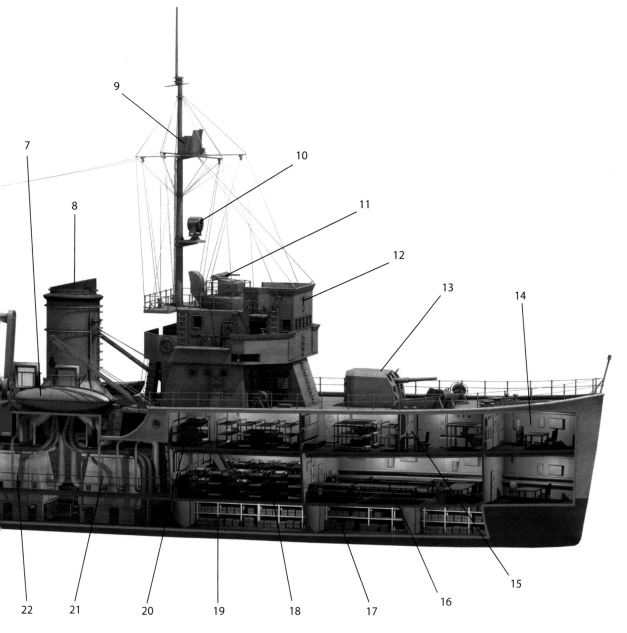

Flotilla	Location	Active
1. MS-Flottille	Baltic/North Sea	1924–45
2. MS-Flottille	Baltic/North Sea	1936–44
3. MS-Flottille	Norway/Baltic	1940–45
4. MS-Flottille	North Sea/Atlantic coast	1939–45
5. MS-Flottille	Norway/North Sea/Baltic	1940–47
6. MS-Flottille	North Sea/Atlantic coast	1939–44
7. MS-Flottille	Baltic/North Sea	1939–45
8. MS-Flottille	Atlantic coast	1941–45
9. MS-Flottille	Norway	1943–47
10. MS-Flottille	Atlantic coast	1943–44
11. MS-Flottille	North Sea/Baltic/Norway	1939–45
12. MS-Flottille	Baltic/North Sea	1939–47
13. MS-Flottille	Baltic/North Sea	1939–42
14. MS-Flottille	North Sea	1939–41
15. MS-Flottille	Baltic/Norway	1939–43
16. MS-Flottille	North Sea/Channel	1939–43
17. MS-Flottille	Baltic/North Sea/Norway	1939–42
18. MS-Flottille	North Sea/Channel/Norway	1939–42
19. MS-Flottille	Baltic/Norway	1939–43
21. MS-Flottille	North Sea/Norway/Baltic	1942–45
22. MS-Flottille	North Sea/Norway/Baltic	1942–45
23. MS-Flottille	Norway/Baltic	1942–47
24. MS-Flottille	Channel Islands	1942–45
25. MS-Flottille	North Sea/Norway/Baltic	1942–45
26. MS-Flottille	French coast	1943–44
27. MS-Flottille	North Sea/Holland	1943–45
28. MS-Flottille	Atlantic coast/Channel	1943–44
29. MS-Flottille	Kattegatt/Skagerak	1943–45
30. MS-Flottille	Norway	1943–45
31. MS-Flottille	Holland/Baltic	1940–45
32. MS-Flottille	Holland	1940–44
34. MS-Flottille	Holland	1940–45
36. MS-Flottille	Holland/Baltic	1940–45
38. MS-Flottille	Channel/Holland/Kattegat	1940–45
40. MS-Flottille	French coast	1940–44
42. MS-Flottille	French coast	1940–44
44. MS-Flottille	French coast	1940–44
46. MS-Flottille	French coast	1942–45
52. MS-Flottille	Norway	1941–45
54. MS-Flottille	Norway	1940–44
56. MS-Flottille	Norway	1940–45
70. MS-Flottille	Mediterranean	1943–44

MOTOR MINESWEEPERS (Räumboote)

The Räumboote (R-boats) were basically small motor minesweepers for inshore work, often doubling as patrol boats or escorts. The first was ordered in 1930 from the firm of Lürssen, the principal manufacturer of S-boats, and indeed there was a resemblance in appearance between R-boats and S-boats, the principal difference being that the former did not carry torpedoes. The first batch consisted of 16 boats, with R1–R8 displacing 43 tons and R9–R16 increased to 52 tons. Armament consisted of only a single heavy machine gun and up to six mines. These earlier boats can be easily identified in photographs by the raised forecastle in contrast to the flush-decked appearance of later boats.

A larger version was introduced in 1934; R17–R24 displaced 120 tons and carried two 2cm guns and up to eight mines. In 1936 a similar, slightly smaller variant but with greater draft appeared, numbered R21 to R40. Both

The officers and crew of a minesweeper mustered on the foredeck for a group photo. The fact that the captain wears the ribbon of the Iron Cross in his buttonhole indicates that the photo was taken after the outbreak of war. By this time most vessels had had the large bronze eagle removed from the front of the bridge for safekeeping, but it is present here. The left-hand lifebelt or fender is lettered '1. Minensuch-Flottille'. (Author's collection)

The dedication to duty of the men of the Sicherungsverbände is reflected by the fact that amongst their number were one winner of the coveted Oakleaves to the Knight's Cross, four Knight's Crosses of the Iron Cross, and 13 German Crosses in Gold. This vessel is Minesweeper M31 of the 5. Minensuchflottille, commanded by Oberleutnant zur See Erwin Leesten, who was awarded the German Cross in Gold on 9 August 1944. (Courtesy Stuart Schultz)

A typical Räumboot. These inshore motor minesweepers were similar in appearance to the early Schnellboote, and indeed manufactured by the same yards, but did not carry torpedoes and had only light armament. Note the T-shape of an eagle-and-swastika emblem below the bridge windows. (Author's collection) displacement to 165 tons. (Deutsches U-Boot-Museum)

1934 and 1936 types remained in production during the war. An even larger version displacing 165 tons was brought into service in 1942; more than 200 were ordered but only around 75 completed. This type had a heavier armament of one 3.7cm and two 2cm guns.

One interesting development of the R-boat arose from the need for small, shallow-draft vessels for use in the narrow fjords of occupied Norway. In October 1940 the officer commanding one unit, Kapitänleutnant Hans Bartels, commissioned the construction of his own highly successful small vessels based on Norwegian fishing boat designs. These 12 boats were called Zwerge ('dwarves') and were to become known as the 'Tigerverband', all vessels flying a pennant bearing a snarling tiger's head over crossed swords. To foster unit morale Bartels even had a small commemorative pin made with this emblem, which was awarded with a special certificate to members of the unit.

Despite his success, higher command did not appreciate junior officers acting on their own initiative in this way, and Bartels found himself posted as first officer to the destroyer Z34.

Räumboote at sea in a heavy chop. These small boats could carry out a variety of duties including escort work, mine-sweeping and sub-chasing. Well over one hundred were built, in classes ranging from 43 tons displacement to 165 tons. (Deutsches U-Boot-Museum)

Operational deployment

The R-boats were organized into 20 flotillas, based as follows:

Flotilla	Location	Active
1. R-Bootsflottille	Baltic/North Sea/Channel	1939–47
2. R-Bootsflottille	North Sea/Channel	1939–44
3. R-Bootsflottille	Baltic/North Sea/Channel/Black Sea	1939–44
4. R-Bootsflottille	North Sea	1940–45
5. R-Bootsflottille	Baltic/North Sea	1939–45
6. R-Bootsflottille	Channel/Mediterranean/Adriatic	1941–45
7. R-Bootsflottille	Channel/North Sea	1940–46
8. R-Bootsflottille	North Sea/Channel	1942–46
9. R-Bootsflottille	Channel	1942–47
10. R-Bootsflottille	Channel	1942–44
11. R-Bootsflottille	Channel	1939–40, 1942–44
12. R–Bootsflottille	Channel/Adriatic/Aegean	1942–45
13. R-Bootsflottille	North Sea	1942–57
14. R–Bootsflottille	Channel/Baltic/North Sea	1943–46
15. R-Bootsflottille	Baltic/North Sea	1944–45
16. R-Bootsflottille	Norway	1944–47
17. R-Bootsflottille	Baltic/Channel	1944–47
21. R-Bootsflottille	Norway	1943–46
25. R-Bootsflottille	North Sea	1943–46
30. R-Bootsflottille	Black Sea	1943–44

OUTPOST or PATROL BOATS (Vorpostenboote)

Vorpostenboote, literally 'outpost boats', was an all-encompassing term used for a wide variety of vessels used for patrol work, forming outer protective screens for convoys and guarding numerous smaller ports. These were primarily former whaling and fishing vessels, and included large numbers of so-called 'booty ships' confiscated or captured from defeated nations. So great was the number and variety of vessels used in these roles that when studying photographs of VP-boats it is difficult to find two that are identical.

These boats were organized in 33 Vorpostenbootflottillen, operating in the following areas:

Area	Flotillas	Area	Flotillas
Baltic	1, 3, 5, 7, 9, 11, 13, 15, 17 & 19	Denmark	9, 10, 16, 18 & 19
North Sea	2, 4, 6, 8, 10, 12, 14, 16, 18 & 20	Norway	63, 64, 65, 66, 67 & 68
France	2, 4, 6, 7, 15 & 18	Mediterranean	70
Holland	8, 11, 13, 14 & 20		

As well as captured and requisitioned former civil vessels, a number of purpose-built types were constructed, based on civilian fishing boat designs, these being known for being extremely sturdy and seaworthy. Such vessels were designated as Kriegsfischcutter, and as well as patrol work they might be used for minesweeping and anti-submarine duties.

SUB-CHASERS (U-Jagd Boote)

Although a small number of dedicated sub-chaser units (U-Bootsjagd Flottillen) were formed, the bulk of anti-submarine operations were carried out by a mixture of minesweepers and VP-boats rather than by vessels specifically designed as anti-submarine warships. It had originally been intended that a range of such purpose-built ships would be constructed, and specifications were drawn up. It was eventually decided, however, that given the size and specification of the proposed vessels, and the issues of shipyard availability and the need not to waste time and resources on unnecessary diversication, that the task of anti-submarine work could be undertaken by existing vessels, particularly the M35 minesweeper. With no specific type of purpose-built sub-chaser vessel, the term was used to describe any boat allocated to such duties.

Operational deployment

Flotilla	Location	Active
1. UJ-Flottille	Black Sea/Baltic	1943–44
2. UJ-Flottille	Adriatic	1944
3. UJ-Flottille	Black Sea/Baltic	1944
11. UJ-Flottille	Baltic/Norway	1939–45
12. UJ-Flottille	North Sea	1939–45
14. UJ-Flottille	Norway/France	1940–45
17. UJ-Flottille	Norway	1939–45
21. UJ-Flottille	Aegean	1941–44
22. UJ-Flottille	Western Mediterranean	1942–45
23. UJ-Flottille	Black Sea	1944

GENERAL PURPOSE BOATS (Mehrzweckboote)

Orders for the production of a new class of escort boat were given in March 1943. The new vessel was effectively to be a more powerful version of the R-boat with heavier armament including, significantly, torpedoes. The new vessel was intended to replace a number of other types such as R-boats and VP-boats. The result was a stylish, 290-ton boat, 52m long and with a 7.2m beam. A single 6-cylinder diesel engine would give it a speed of just 14 knots, sufficient for its role of escorting slower vessels. Armament consisted of 2x 8.8cm, one 3.7cm and eight 2cm flak guns. Two torpedo tubes were fitted, emerging from the hull near the bow in a somewhat similar manner to those on S-boats.

This shot clearly shows that the origins for the design of typical Vorpostenboote came from fishing boats. These smaller types were in fact also referred to as Kriegsfischkutter. (Deutsches U-Boot-Museum)

It was originally intended that 12 boats would be built by the Stülcken yard in Hamburg, but in the event only one was ever completed, MZ1. This boat was built in a conventional manner, but it was intended that future boats would be assembled from pre-fabricated sections. MZ1 was launched on 16 April 1944 and was well received. Had Germany's military and industrial situation not been so bad by this date it is likely that significant numbers of this new type would have been constructed, but all that existed by the end of the war was MZ1 and the keels of three more partially constructed boats.

Records of MZ1's use and eventual fate are virtually non-existent. It is believed that she was captured by British forces when Eckernförde fell, but there seems to be no record of what befell her.

BARRIER-BREAKERS (Sperrbrecher)

The purpose of the Sperrbrecher, rather than to clear minefields, was to escort ships into and out of German-held ports along cleared paths through defensive minefield barriers, and to detonate any mines that might have been laid by the enemy in these clear paths.

Most Sperrbrecher began their lives as merchant vessels, and were crewed by merchant seamen with a small cadre of naval personnel. These were termed 'Special Purpose Merchant Ships' (Handelsdampfer zb V). Others were crewed entirely by naval personnel. Both German-built and captured foreign vessels were pressed into service as Sperrbrecher. It was typical for a Sperrbrecher to have its hold filled with buoyant material to help keep it afloat should it run into a mine, and for the bows to be significantly strengthened. Nevertheless the detonation of a powerful mine could easily break the back of a ship, so service on this type of vessel must have required strong nerves on the part of its crew. Photos of Sperrbrecher will often show a metal beam set just forward of the bow, intended to detonate any mine before it touched the hull itself.

A larger Vorpostenboot, this time in pale grey livery, with her main armament on a platform at the bow. Her 'fishing trawler' lines are still clear. (Deutsches U-Boot-Museum)

Armament on Sperrbrecher varied; as they were never expected to engage enemy surface ships it tended to consist primarily of anti-aircraft guns, but these might be numerous. Typical armament in the second half of the war might comprise 2x 10.5cm, 6x 3.7cm and 14x 2cm guns. In addition, many Sperrbrecher were equipped with barrage balloons.

This interesting shot of a Sperrbrecher in harbour shows just how effective disruptive camouflage schemes could be. The use of the black German cross emblem on the side of the superstructure is most unusual on ships. (Author's collection)

Operational deployment

Barrier-breakers were organized into a total of seven Sperrbrecherflottillen, as follows; like the minesweepers, more than one unit remained in service after the war, making safe the waters around Europe's coasts:

Flotilla	Location	Active
1. Sperrbrecherflottille	Baltic/German Bight	1940–46
2. Sperrbrecherflottille	Channel/Bay of Biscay	1939–44
3. Sperrbrecherflottille	Baltic	1940–46
4. Sperrbrecherflottille	Channel	1941–43
5. Sperrbrecherflottille	*never operational; existed only 1 month*	
6. Sperrbrecherflottille	Bay of Biscay	1941–44
8. Sperrbrecherflottille	North Sea/Channel	1941–45

1: Raumboot

A typical R-boat from the batch numbered R73 to R88, manufactured in about 1941. These fast, manoeuvrable, shallow-draft boats became the 'maids of all work' among the Kriegsmarine's coastal craft, but were predominantly used as escorts or inshore minesweepers.

2: Vorpostenboot

This is but one example of what appears to have been a myriad of variants of these 'outpost boats'. One common feature is that almost all of the types used bore a strong resemblance to the basic design of a fishing boat, with a high forecastle (usually with a gun platform) and a relatively tall funnel. These robust little boats were capable of working in the roughest of seas. Many survived the war to take part in post-war mine clearing.

3: Flottenbegleiter

Only ten examples were produced of this unsuccessful class of vessel; the illustration shows one of the first six, built at the Germaniawerft yard in Kiel. The remaining four, built by Blohm & Voss in Hamburg and the Kriegsmarine Werft in Wilhelmshaven, were very similar, but with marginally shorter funnels and a slightly different layout to the superstructure amidships.

4: German state yacht '*Aviso Grille*'

For a yacht *Grille* was powerfully armed. Her three 10.5cm gun turrets were supplemented by two twin 3.7cm flak mounts just aft of the funnel, as well as four single 2cm mounts. The rakish lines of *Grille* were seen at numerous naval regattas before the war, and she hosted many foreign dignitaries. Although she is often referred to as 'Hitler's' yacht, in fact he rarely visited her. After the outbreak of war she served in numerous roles, including as a 'target' ship for training the crews of torpedo-carrying aircraft.

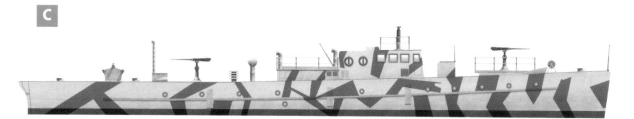

1: Raumboot

2: Vorpostenboot

3: Flottenbegleiter

4: German state yacht '*Aviso Grille*'

ESCORT BOATS (Geleitboote)

A distinction must be drawn between improvized and purpose-built escorts. A class of fleet escorts (Flottenbegleiter) were planned and built, their pennant numbers being prefixed with 'F'. However, only ten were ever constructed, as follows:

Shipyard	Vessels	Total
Germaniawerft, Kiel	F1–F6	6
Blohm & Voss, Hamburg	F7–8	2
Kriegsmarinewerft, Wilhelmshaven	F9–10	2

Specifications:			
Length	68m	Powerplant	2x 14,000hp turbines
Beam	8.7m	Top speed	18 knots
Displacement	870 tons	Endurance	5,000 nautical miles
Armament	1x 10.5cm gun, 1x 3.7cm flak, 4x 2cm flak; 4x depth charge launchers; up to 30 mines	Crew	24

The first was launched in December 1935 and the last by March 1938. The principal purpose for which they were designed was to act as an inner escort screen for the 'pocket battleships' *Deutschland*, *Admiral Graf Spee* and *Admiral Scheer*. Due to technical problems with the type of high-pressure boilers installed in these vessels, they were not considered successful and no more were ordered. They were organized into two flotillas as follows:

Flotilla	Vessels
1. Geleitflottille	F1, 2, 5, 6, 9 & 10
2. Geleitflottille	F3, 4, 7 & 8

Deployments

Due to their limitations, it was decided that these vessels could best be employed as minesweepers; but problems during exercises raised questions over their speed, manoeuvrability and endurance as well as the reliability of their engines, and led to the disbandment of 2. Geleitflottille. The Geleitboote were finally judged to be of so little effective value that even before the outbreak of war it was decided to delegate them to various non-combat duties, as follows:

Flotilla	Duty
F1	To be allocated as a command ship to Führer der Minensuchboote Ost
F2, F4 & F7	To be converted into torpedo recovery vessels
F3 & F6	To be converted into tenders, with most armament removed and extra accommodation added
F5, F8, F9 & F10	To be allocated to the Anti-Submarine Warfare School as training vessels

However, the outbreak of war in September 1939 put paid to these plans. Under wartime conditions the Navy had to make the best it could of these boats; but by December, F9 had been lost when torpedoed by a British submarine, and the others had performed so badly that the plan to remove them from operational service was revived. Any thoughts of trying to refit and improve these boats was quickly discarded as a waste of up dockyard time and resources.

Accordingly, F2, F5, F7, F8 and F10 were simply handed over to the U-boat arm for use as torpedo recovery vessels and submarine escorts. F1 was allocated to the Führer der Zerstörer as a tender/command vessel; F3, allocated to the Führer der Minensuchboote in the same role, was sunk by rocket-firing aircraft in May 1945. F4 served as a trials vessel with Sperrversuchskommando and Torpedoversuchsanhalt, but returned to minelaying in 1944. F6 took part in the attack on Norway, allocated to the Führer der Minensuchboote (West); she saw service in minelaying and escort duties throughout the war, eventually being sunk by Allied aircraft during an attack on Wilhelmshaven in April 1945.

Despite their serious limitations these ships were relatively fortunate in that six of the ten survived the war, and a number served on under the less demanding needs of peacetime; indeed, F7 served in the Soviet Navy until at least 1956.

Although these purpose-built Flottenbegleiter were a complete failure, the concept of allocating vessels into units specifically tasked with escort work survived them. In all seven flotillas were created, deployed operationally as follows:

Flotilla	Location	Active
1. Geleitflottille (reformed)	Adriatic	1944–45
2. Geleitflottille (reformed)	Adriatic	1944–45
3. Geleitflottille	Mediterranean	1943–44
4. Geleitflottille	Mediterranean	1943–44
5. Geleitflottille	Baltic	1945
30. Geleitflottille	Black Sea	1943–44
31. Geleitflottille	Black Sea	1942–44

Additional small units under the control of the Sicherungsverbände included:

Netzsperrverband Units that maintained the boom defence nets around German ports and naval bases. The vessels were classed as Netzleger (netlayers) and Netztender. The flotillas into which these units were formed were designated by area rather than number, i.e. Netzsperrflottille Nord.

Hafenschutzflottillen Harbour protection flotillas were generally formed of small craft such as armed trawlers and armed tugboats and, as the name suggests, were permanently based in ports to protect the installations. There were three such flotillas based in major German naval bases: Hafenschutzflottille Cuxhaven, Hafenschutzflottille Wilhelmshaven and Hafenschutzflottille Borkum.

POST-WAR ACTIVITIES OF THE SICHERUNGSVERBÄNDE

At the end of hostilities in May 1945 huge amounts of work remained to be done in clearing mines from European coastal waters.

A large number of Kriegsmarine personnel remained in service between August 1945 and December 1947, in the Deutsche Minenräumdienstleitung

(German Mine Sweeping Administration, GMSA), continuing to wear their Kriegsmarine uniforms and insignia – though of course with the swastikas removed. This organization was under British control; although many personnel were issued new GMSA paybooks, a large number of original Third Reich-period issued books continued in use, and examples may be found with Royal Navy entries.

From January 1948, German minesweeping activities passed to the Deutsche Minenräumverband based in Cuxhaven. This comprised around 45 officers and just over 500 men, all of whom were volunteers, under the ultimate authority of the Allied Control Commission. These men cleared mines from coastal waters until June 1951 and the creation of the Seegrenzschutz (Sea Border Defence service), which led ultimately to the foundation of the Bundesmarine (Federal German Navy).

The minesweeping service therefore presents a unique situation, in which a German sailor might have virtually unbroken sea service from the days of the Kriegsmarine through to the Federal Navy of West Germany.

TORPEDO BOATS

To British and American ears the term torpedo boat conjures up images of the MTB (Motor Torpedo Boat) or PT-boat (Patrol Torpedo Boat) – a small, fast, motor-launch type of vessel relying on its high speed to survive attacks on enemy shipping. Nothing could be further removed from the reality of a German Torpedoboote, which in fact was a small destroyer akin to the US Destroyer Escort.

On the outbreak of war the bulk of the Kriegsmarine's torpedo boat fleet was made up of vessels that had been built in the second half of the 1920s and were already somewhat dated. All were built at the Marinewerft in Wilhelmshaven; the first batch of six were designated as the 'Raubvogel' (Wild Bird) class, and named accordingly as follows: *Möwe* (Seagull), *Seeadler* (Sea Eagle), *Greif* (Griffon Vulture), *Albatros*, *Kondor* and *Falke* (Falcon). A second batch of six, the 'Raubtier' (Wild Animal) class, consisted of the following: *Wolf*, *Iltis* (Polecat), *Luchs* (Lynx), *Tiger*, *Jaguar* and *Leopard*.

Specifications – M23, Raubvogel class:			
Length	87m	Powerplant	2x Schichau 23,000hp turbines
Beam	8.3m	Top speed	33 knots
Displacement	898 tons	Endurance	1,800 nautical miles
Armament	3x 10.5cm guns, 4x 3.7cm flak, 4x 2cm flak; 6x torpedo tubes; 4x depth charge launchers; up to 30 mines	Crew	120–130

Specifications – M24, Raubtier class:			
Length	92.6m	Powerplant	2x Schichau 23,000hp turbines
Beam	8.6m	Top speed	34 knots
Displacement	933 tons	Endurance	2,000 nautical miles
Armament	3x 10.5cm guns, 4x 3.7cm flak, 4x 2cm flak; 6x torpedo tubes; 4x depth charge launchers; up to 30 mines	Crew	120–130

Type 35 torpedo boats

Despite various improvements and refits it was clear that a more modern type would be required, and in 1935 a new design was approved for construction. Between 1936 and 1942 a total of 21 of these M35 types (including an improved but basically similar variant introduced in 1937) were built. This class were not named but identified by a pennant number prefixed with 'T' for Torpedoboot:

Shipyard	Vessels	Total
Schichau, Elbing	T1–4, T9–10, T13–21	15
Deschimag, Bremen	T5–6, T11–12	6

Specifications – M35 class:			
Length	84m	Powerplant	2x Wagner 31,000hp turbines
Beam	8.6m	Top speed	34.5 knots
Displacement	859 tons	Endurance	1,070 nautical miles
Armament	1x 10.5cm gun, 1x 3.7cm flak, 2x 2cm flak; 6x torpedo tubes; 4x depth charge launchers; up to 30 mines	Crew	117

Operational deployment

There were nine torpedo boat flotillas numbered sequentially 1–7 and 9–10, the 8th Flotilla never becoming operational. Their deployment was as follows:

Flotilla	Deployment
1. Torpedobootflottille (formed pre-war)	1939–April 1941: North Sea and English Channel April–Aug 1941: Baltic Aug 1941: Stood down
2. Torpedobootflottille (formed pre-war)	1940–41: Operational in Channel 1941: Operational in Baltic 1942–43: Defensive minelaying in Western waters 1943–44: Training flotilla 1944–45: Escort service in Baltic
3. Torpedobootflottille (formed April 1941)	1941–42: Working-up and training exercises 1942: Minelaying in Western waters 1943–44: Training duties with Torpedo School, and combined operations with U-boats in Baltic 1944–45: Patrol and security duties in eastern Baltic and Skagerak
4.Torpedobootflottille (formed Feb 1943)	1943–44: Minelaying and escort duties in Western waters Apr 1944: Stood down
5. Torpedobootflottille (formed pre-war)	1939–40: Defensive minelaying, escort duties and anti-shipping operations in Western waters 1940: Invasion of Norway; escort and security duties in Skagerak 1941–44: Escort duties; offensive and defensive minelaying in Western waters 1944: Based on French Channel coast; all ships destroyed during Normandy invasion campaign 1944–45: Re-formed; served in Finnish waters and eastern Baltic escorting evacuation operations
6. Torpedobootflottille (formed pre-war)	1939–40: Minelaying, escort and anti-shipping operations in Western waters 1940–41: Security and escort duties during invasion of Norway; minelaying and escort duty Feb 1941: Stood down
7. Torpedobootflottille (formed Nov 1943)	1943–44: Operational in Finnish waters, and defensive minelaying in Baltic Aug 1944: Stood down
9. Torpedobootflottille (formed late summer 1943)	1943–44: Operational in Aegean Oct 1944: Stood down
10. Torpedobootflottille (formed Jan 1944)	1944–45: Operational in Mediterranean

Operational history – M23 & M24 boats

All these torpedo boats were active during the Spanish Civil War as part of Germany's 'non-intervention' patrols. All vessels of both classes were also involved in escort work for the invasion fleet during the attack on Norway in April 1940. By the end of that campaign four of the 12 vessels had been lost, and the remaining eight were thereafter grouped together in 5. Torpedobootsflottille. During the second half of 1940 the flotilla was heavily involved in minelaying operations in the English Channel, and also in 'hit and run' attacks on British merchant shipping.

Five of these warships – *Seeadler*, *Kondor*, *Falke*, *Iltis* and *Jaguar* – were also involved in Operation 'Cerberus' (the 'Channel Dash'), escorting the battleships *Scharnhorst* and *Gneisenau* and the heavy cruiser *Prinz Eugen* during their run eastwards through the English Channel in February 1942; *Jaguar* was severely damaged by British aircraft during this operation. On 14/15 May 1942, *Seeadfler*, *Iltis*, *Kondor* and *Falke* formed part of the escort screen for the auxiliary cruiser *Stier* as she broke out into the Atlantic

This pre-war shot shows the 1920s vintage torpedo boat *Albatros* (identified by the letters 'AT' on the bow) sporting the typical black paint scheme widely used on smaller vessels pre-war. The crew lined up for this photo seem to be 56 ratings in whites, 11 petty-officers in blue jackets and white trousers, and five officers in blue uniforms – about half her complement. (Author's collection)

through the Channel. The German ships came under fire from both long-range coastal artillery at Dover and from British MTBs, and both *Iltis* and *Seeadler* were sunk.

The remainder of these elderly boats continued to give good service until the summer of 1944, when they were all destroyed in Allied bombing raids conected with the Normandy invasion. The individual fates of the M23 and M24 class were as follows:

Vessel	Launched	Commissioned	Fate
Möwe	March 1926	Oct 1926	sunk at moorings in Le Havre during air raid, 15 June 1944
Seeadler	July 1926	May 1927	sunk in action with British MTBs in the Channel, 13 May 1942
Albatros	July 1926	May 1927	beached May 1940 after being crippled by Norwegian coastal artillery
Greif	July 1926	March 1927	sunk in Seine estuary during air raid, 23 May 1944
Kondor	Sept 1926	July 1927	sunk at moorings in Le Havre during air raid, 31 July 1944
Falke	Sept 1926	Aug 1927	sunk at moorings in Le Havre during air raid, 15 June 1944
Wolf	Oct 1927	Nov 1928	sunk by British mine off Dunkirk, 8 January 1941
Iltis	Oct 1927	Oct 1928	sunk in action with British MTBs in the Channel, 13 May 1942
Luchs	March 1928	April 1929	sunk in North Sea by British submarine HMS *Swordfish*, 26 July 1940
Tiger	March 1928	Jan 1929	sunk in collision with German destroyer *Max Schulz*, 25 August 1939
Jaguar	March 1928	June 1929	sunk at moorings in Le Havre during air raid, 15 June 1944
Leopard	March 1928	June 1929	sunk in collision with German minelayer *Preussen*, 1 April 1940

Operational history – M35 boats

The more modern torpedo boat designs were certainly more stylish in appearance that their elderly forerunners, but the use of high-pressure turbines as fitted in the larger German destroyers resulted in their suffering similar technical problems. They were also poor seagoing vessels, and could not be used for minelaying except in calm weather; one of their perceived positive points had been their anticipated ability to carry out high-speed, short-range minelaying sorties. In addition to their other shortcomings, they also had relatively light armament. Most of them were relegated to non-combat duties, assigned to U-boat training flotillas in the Baltic.

A helmsman at the wheel on the bridge of a torpedo boat. This area was far from spacious, and the dark colour scheme must have made visibility somewhat problematic during the hours of darkness. (Deutsches U-Boot-Museum)

The M35 torpedo boats first became operational in late 1940 with 1. Torpedobootsflottille, which had been created a year earlier; it had taken this length of time to deliver the boats allocated to the flotilla in serviceable condition following numerous powerplant failures.

This flotilla was disbanded in August 1941; during its short life T1 was severely damaged after running aground, T2 had to spend several months in dock for repairs when she was damaged by a bomb dropped by a British aircraft while escorting a minelaying mission; T3 was sunk during a bombing raid on Le Havre (though she was later raised); and T6 was lost when she ran onto a mine.

The 2. Torpedobootsflottille began operations in the summer of 1940. Shortly after the flotilla moved to France, T11 was severely damaged in a bombing attack and subsequently spent several months in repair dock. Availability of operational boats was a constant problem, since regular visits to the dockyard for repairs were required. The flotilla did perform some useful tasks, particularly in the escort role, and was involved in the successful 'Channel Dash'; but from mid 1943 to mid 1944 no operational sorties were undertaken. T2 and T4 were sunk during a bombing raid on Bremen, and although refloated they never returned to service. Although T3 did succeed in sinking a Soviet submarine in January 1945, the late stages of the war were spent on escorting convoys in the Baltic; during one such mission both T3 and T5 were sunk by mines laid by a Soviet submarine.

M39 class

The largely unsuccessful M35 class would be followed by an even larger type known as the M39 or Fleet Torpedo Boats (Flotten-Torpedoboote). Construction was again shared between Schichau and Deschimag, but in the event only the batch of 16 awarded to the Schichau yard at Elbing were completed, and numbered T22–36.

Specifications – M39 Flottentorpedoboot:			
Length	102.5m	Top speed	30 knots
Beam	10m	Endurance	2,400 nautical miles
Displacement	294 tons	Crew	198
Armament	4x 10.5cm guns, 4x 3.7cm flak, 2x 2cm flak; 6x torpedo tubes; 4x depth charge launchers; up to 50 mines		

Operational history

After the problems suffered by the M35/37 type the M39 'Elbing' class boats were a massive improvement, and true multi-role warships rather than simply torpedo boats. Bigger and heavier than their predecessors, this class was almost a hybrid between the smaller torpedo boats and the larger destroyers; they were seaworthy, fast and highly manoeuvrable. Much of the work performed by this class was on escort duties and they were certainly capable

D **TORPEDO BOATS**

1: Raubvogel class

Shown here in its early 1930s form, this torpedo boat is finished in the typical black early colour scheme. The foremost and sternmost open gun mounts have been replaced by enclosed turrets; the raised stern mount – only marginally more protected in heavy seas – is still open to the elements. By the late stages of the war the surviving members of this early class of torpedo boats had all of their main armament in turrets, carried radar antennae on both masts, and mounted increased anti-aircraft armament.

2: M39 Flottentorpedoboot

The more rakish lines of this class are evident. Note the additional main armament turret mounted admidships, giving this type a total of four 10.5cm guns – as many as some full-size destroyers. Anti-aircraft armament consisted of two twin 3.7cm guns as well as single and quadruple 2cm flak mounts. With two triple torpedo tubes, these were very powerfully armed for small warships.

(Details, left) Typical open gun mount found on the early torpedo boats. The weapon is a 10.5cm L/45, introduced in 1932 but based on a design dating back to before World War I. It had a rate of fire of 15 rounds per minute, firing a 24kg shell at a muzzle velocity of 780 metres per second.

(Details, right) Now enclosed in a turret, the main armament fitted to later types of torpedo boat – the 10.5cm L/45 C/32 – was basically the same as the earlier piece. Note the raised armoured flap, dropped when not in use to protect the delicate sighting optics.

TORPEDO BOATS

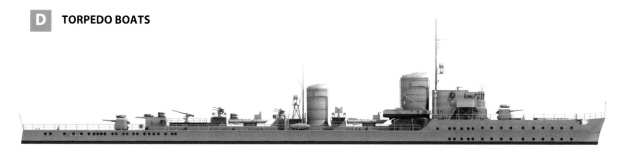

1: Raubvogel class

2: M39 Flottentorpedoboot

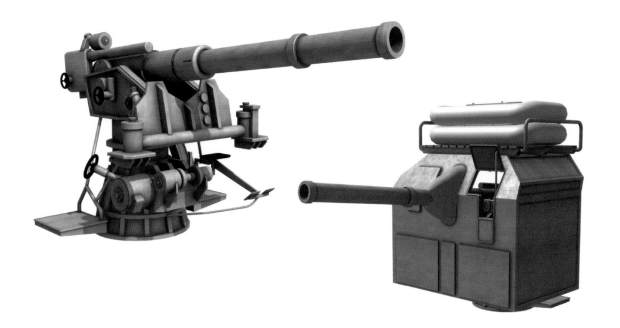

A Raubvogel class torpedo boat in pale grey livery, a scheme carried by almost all Kriegsmarine vessels by 1939. The identifying letters are no longer displayed on the bow. (Deutsches U-Boot-Museum)

of giving a good account of themselves. Since most of the ports in the West had been lost by the time the last five were commissioned, those spent their active careers in the Baltic.

In Western waters in late 1943 the Elbings were involved in escorting a blockade-runner carrying a cargo of critically important war material back home to Germany from Japan. The convoy was attacked by the British light cruiser HMS *Charybdis*, accompanied by a number of destroyers. The German torpedo boats immediately went on to the offensive and launched torpedoes at the British cruiser; at least two hit their target, leaving the warship dead in the water. Torpedoes were also launched at the accompanying destroyers, scoring a direct hit on HMS *Limbourne*. The remaining British warships withdrew, and the German convoy reached port unscathed. The Royal Navy had learned a hard lesson about the potential of these powerful torpedo boats. Only when they decided to have their cruisers stand off and direct the faster destroyers by radar, whilst using their own heavy guns against the torpedo boats at long range, did they achieve greater success. The fate of individual boats of the M39 class was as follows:

Vessel	Commissioned	Fate
T22	Feb 1942	sunk 18 August 1944 with loss of 143 crew when she ran onto one of her own mines
T23	June 1942	survived the war; taken into service by the British in 1946
T24	Oct 1942	sunk with loss of 18 crew by British air attack, 24 August 1944
T25	Dec 1942	sunk with loss of 85 crew during engagement in Bay of Biscay with British destroyers HMS *Glasgow* and *Enterprise*, 28 December 1943
T26	Feb 1943	lost with 90 crew in same engagement as T25
T27	April 1943	ran aground after engagement with Canadian destroyer off Breton coast, later destroyed by Allied aircraft; most of her crew survived
T28	June 1942	survived the war; taken into service by the British in 1945
T29	Aug 1943	sunk with loss of 137 crew by gunfire and torpedoes from British cruiser HMS *Black Prince* and destroyers HMS *Haida*, *Huron*, *Ashanti* and *Athebascan*, 26 April 1944
T30	Oct 1943	sunk with loss of 114 crew when she ran into German minefield, 18 August 1944
T31	Feb 1944	sunk with loss of 82 crew by torpedo from Soviet MTB, 20 June 1944
T32	May 1944	sunk with loss of 137 crew when she ran into German minefield, 18 August 1944 (see T30)
T33	June 1944	survived the war; taken into service by the Soviet Navy
T34	Aug 1944	sunk with loss of 62 crew off Cap Arcona by torpedo from Soviet submarine L3, 20 November 1944
T35	Oct 1944	survived the war; taken into service by US Navy
T36	Dec 1944	sunk with loss of 63 crew by mine and Soviet aircraft off Usedom, 4 May 1945

The more rakish appearance of the M39 Elbing class Flottentorpedoboot was not deceptive; this class were a great improvement on their predecessors, being excellent sea-boats and heavily armed. However, only 16 were ever built, and the last five delivered were limited to operations in the Baltic through the earlier loss of Western ports in 1944. (Deutsches U-Boot-Museum)

Britain, the USA, France, the USSR and Denmark all made good use of captured torpedo boats post-war. As well as German-built torpedo boats a number of captured ships – predominantly Norwegian, French and Italian – were also taken into service by the Kriegsmarine, the French and Italian vessels being predominantly used in the Mediterranean with the majority being lost in action.

FLEET AUXILIARY SUPPLY SHIPS (Tross-schiffe)

In common with other nations, the German Navy commandeered many merchant vessels for military use. These were classified into a whole range of supply ship classes, many of which retained their original merchant navy crews on temporary secondment to the Kriegsmarine for the duration of hostilities. A typical example was the *Jan Wellem*, the mothership of the German whaling fleet, which served with its original merchant navy crew in the invasion of Norway and was severely damaged at Narvik.

However, there were also a small number of purpose-built fleet auxiliaries of the *Dithmarschen* class, produced in 1936 and 1937. It had originally been intended that these ships could double as auxiliary cruisers; it was later decided that their role as supply ships was too valuable to divert them onto combat duties as auxiliary warships, but their original intended role was reflected in the manner in which their main armament was concealed behind collapsible panels.

As indicated by their official designation as Flottentross-schiffe, these vessels came under the control of Fleet command via the Chef des Tross-schiffverbandes headquartered in Wilhelmshaven, and not the Sicherungsverbände. These ships would typically carry fuel, ammunition, food, machine parts and even mail from home. The crews were Kriegsmarine personnel, but were recruited for the Navy from experienced merchant seamen who, already possessing all the seamanship skills required, simply needed to be put through an abbreviated military training programme.

A total of five new supply ships were built: *Dithmarschen*, *Uckermark* (originally *Altmark*), *Nordmark* (originally *Westerwald*), *Ermland* and *Franken*. Only *Dithmarschen* and *Nordmark* survived the war, the former serving with the US Navy until scrapped in 1960, and the latter with the Royal Navy until 1955.

The supply ship (Tross-schiff) *Tannenfels*, which resupplied several of the auxiliary cruisers on their many successful wartime raiding cruises. Note that – somewhat unusually for a supply ship – she is carrying a floatplane (silhouetted behind the funnel), but this was most likely a replacement she was transporting to one of the commerce raiders. (Deutsches U-Boot-Museum)

Specifications for the class:				
Length	178m	Powerplant	2 x Wagner turbines
Beam	22m	Top speed	21 knots
Displacement	20,860 tons	Endurance	12,500 nautical miles
Armament	3x 15cm guns, 2x 3.7cm flak, 4x 2cm flak	Crew	100–200

Operational history
Dithmarschen

Dithmarschen began her career as a supply tanker for German warships involved in non–intervention patrols during the Spanish Civil War, on the conclusion of which she went into dry dock for repairs and refitting. She returned to active service in June 1940, providing refuelling for the battleships *Scharnhorst* and *Gneisenau*, the heavy cruiser *Admiral Hipper* and numerous destroyers during Operation 'Juno', an attempt to interdict supply movements for the British force fighting in Norway. In November 1940 she was scheduled to accompany the pocket battleship *Admiral Scheer* on operations but was forced to return to port due to engine problems.

Bad luck continued to dog the *Dithmarschen*, and in January 1941, when setting off on a further refuelling mission for *Scharnhorst* and *Gneisenau*, she ran aground. Out of action for some time during repairs, she returned to service in 1943, acting as a supply tanker for Kriegsmarine ships operating from Norwegian harbours. At the end of the war *Dithmarschen* passed to the US Navy, who renamed her *Conecuh*. She served for ten years, being retired to the reserves in 1956 and finally scrapped in 1960.

Altmark/Uckermark

On the outbreak of war *Altmark* was operating in the South Atlantic, as the supply ship for the *Admiral Graf Spee*. After the scuttling of that raider *Altmark* successfully ran the Allied blockade into what were assumed to be relatively safe waters, still carrying a number of

The Blockade-Breaker Badge, showing a merchant vessel, its prow adorned with the eagle-and-swastika, breaking through a chain symbolizing the Allied blockade. (Author's collection)

E

RAUBTIER CLASS TORPEDO BOAT IN ACTION
12 FEBRUARY 1942

Once the Low Countries and France had fallen in May–June 1940 and Germany took control of their ports on the coasts of the North Sea, English Channel and Atlantic, torpedo boats operated from the North Sea right down into the Bay of Biscay. They were often involved in fierce engagements with British warships; but the most significant single operation in which the torpedo boats took part was the famous 'Channel Dash', when the battlecruisers *Scharnhorst* and *Gneisenau* and the heavy cruiser *Prinz Eugen* broke out from Brest and, thanks to a brilliantly executed plan of continuous sea and air support, sailed safely up the Channel to return to dockyard facilities in German ports. The belated and unsuccessful attempts by British naval and air forces to stop them were costly for the RN Fleet Air Arm and the RAF.

This plate shows a torpedo boat of the escort force under attack from Spitfire fighter aircraft. The boat is sporting an interesting 'splinter'-style disruptive camouflage scheme in dark grey and medium blue-grey over her pre-war plain pale grey finish. During this operation the torpedo boat *Jaguar* suffered the highest casualties on the German side – just one man killed and one wounded. Fast and manoeuvrable even in heavy seas, this class of boat carried a 3.7cm flak gun and anything between two and 12 light 2cm flak guns. Their anti-aircraft armament was continuously upgraded throughout the war, and a torpedo boat at speed thus presented a target both difficult to hit and capable of putting up a robust defence.

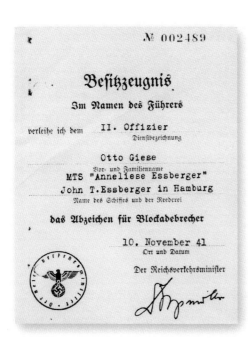

The award document for the Blockade-Breaker Badge awarded to Otto Giese. Note the interesting additional line below the ship name MTS *Anneliese Essberger* – 'John T.Essberger in Hamburg' – the shipping line to which the ship belonged. The date, 10 November 41, is a month before the US entry into the war. On reaching Germany, Giese transferred to the U-boat branch, and served at one point with the top 'ace' Wolfgang Lüth. (Otto Giese)

captured merchant seamen who had been transferred from the *Graf Spee*. However, radio traffic from the Altmark had been intercepted by the British, and she was located by the Royal Navy destroyer HMS *Cossack* off the coast of then-neutral Norway. On the appearance of *Cossack* on 16 February 1940 she ran for refuge in Norwegian territorial waters, but the destroyer followed her and boarded her; a number of allegedly unarmed German sailors were shot while the boarding party released the prisoners. It is believed that this event led Hitler to suspect Norwegian collusion with Britain and to hasten his plans for the invasion of Norway.

On her return to Germany the *Altmark* was renamed as the *Uckermark*, and subsequently served in the Pacific and Indian Oceans as supply ship for the auxiliary cruiser *Thor*. In November 1942, while moored in Yokahama in Japan, *Uckermark* was torn apart by a huge explosion believed to have been caused by sparks during cleaning work on her fuel tanks.

Westerwald/Nordmark

On the outbreak of war *Westerwald* was serving as supply tanker for the pocket battleship *Deutschland*; after returning to Germany in December 1939 she was renamed *Nordmark*. After taking part in the invasion of Norway, she was damaged in an air raid in July 1940 and spent two months undergoing repairs. Her next task was to serve as supply tanker for the *Admiral Scheer*, undergoing a long and successful cruise in which she covered more than 33,600 miles during over 250 days at sea. From March 1942 until the end of the war, *Nordmark* served as a supply tanker for German naval units in Norway.

After the cessation of hostilities she was taken into the Royal Navy, where she served as the *Bulowayo*. She was scrapped in 1955.

Ermland

Launched in 1939, *Ermland* was commissioned into the Kriegsmarine in September 1940. She was despatched to act as a supply tanker for the battleships *Scharnhorst* and *Gneisenau*, but was recalled when those warships were unable to break out into the Atlantic. From January to March 1941 she served them during Operation 'Berlin', a raiding cruise against Allied merchant shipping. Shortly after the conclusion of this mission *Ermland* was ordered to sea again to support the damaged *Bismarck* as she struggled to reach the safety of occupied France, but the tanker was recalled when the news of *Bismarck's* sinking was received. Her relatively short career ended in September 1942 when she ran onto a mine, and had to go into dry dock for repairs. Whilst in port in Nantes she was severely damaged during an air raid in September 1943, and rendered unserviceable. She was eventually sunk as a block-ship at Nantes in August 1944.

Franken

Franken was not completed until September 1943, and spent her war rather uneventfully in the Baltic on supply operations. She suffered a direct hit when bombed by Soviet aircraft on 8 April 1945, broke in half, and rapidly sank.

TENDERS/ESCORTS

Flotillas of smaller vessels such as S-boats and U-boats, which often moved location through various ports in Germany and, during wartime, through occupied Europe, needed a larger support vessel providing feeding, medical treatment, supplies and accommodation facilities. This requirement led to the construction of a number of purpose-built tenders; the exact nomenclature used often changed, though the basic purpose remained. The designation as a Tender or Escort related to the type of duties performed rather than the type of ship. Tenders were classed as either simply 'Tender', or Flottentender, Stationstender, Unterseebootstender, etc. As an example of how designations might change for the same ship, the Saar will be found referred to as both a Fleet Tender (Flottentender *Saar*) and as a Submarine Escort Ship (U-Bootsbegleitschiff *Saar*).

The Flottentender *Gazelle*, one of many small auxiliary vessels used by the Kriegsmarine. During wartime they were often employed as command ships, for escort or minesweeping duties. (Deutsches U-Boot-Museum)

Examples of some of the more important vessels of this type would include the following:

Wilhelm Bauer

Built by Howaldtswerke in Kiel, *Wilhelm Bauer* was the first ship of her class to be completed; she was launched in December 1938 and commissioned in April 1940. In July she became the depot ship for 27. Unterseebootsflottille, and in March 1945 for 25. U-flottille. She was bombed and sunk on 8 April 1945, and raised and scrapped in 1950.

Specifications:			
Length	132.7m	Powerplant	4x MAN diesels
Beam	16m	Top speed	20 knots
Displacement	5,600 tons	Endurance	9,000 nautical miles
Armament	2x twin 10.5cm guns, 1x 4cm flak, 2x 3.7cm flak, 4x 2cm flak	Crew	289

This photo shows First Officer Otto Giese aboard the blockade-runner *Anneliese Essberger*. After supplying auxiliary cruisers in the Far East, she broke through the Allied blockade and returned to Germany safely. (Otto Giese)

Waldemar Kophamel

Launched in May 1939 and commissioned in October 1940, her first allotted task was as depot ship for 27. Unterseebootsflottille. In February 1941 she took over responsibility for 24. U-flottille, before returning to her original charges in February 1942. Bombed and sunk by Allied aircraft in December 1944, she was raised by the Soviets in 1950 and taken on strength by the Soviet Navy, serving as the *Kuban*; she was eventually scrapped in 1978.

Specifications:			
Length	132.7m	Powerplant	4x MAN diesels
Beam	16m	Top speed	20 knots
Displacement	5,600 tons	Endurance	9,000 nautical miles
Armament	2x twin 10.5cm guns, 1x 4cm flak, 2x 3.7cm flak, 4x 2cm flak	Crew	289

Otto Wünsche

Launched in May 1940 but not commissioned until November 1943, *Otto Wünsche* was the last of the Howaldtswerke-built *Wilhelm Bauer* class. Her assignment until just before the end of the war was as depot ship with 27. Unterseebootsflottille, joining 26. U-flottille thereafter. She survived the war, being taken into service by the Soviet Navy as the *Pechora*; she ended her life as an accommodation ship, but was not finally scrapped until 1977.

Specifications:			
Length	139m	Powerplant	4x MAN diesels
Beam	16m	Top speed	21 knots
Displacement	5,900 tons	Endurance	9,000 nautical miles
Armament	2x twin 10.5cm guns, 1x 4cm flak, 2x 3.7cm flak, 4x 2cm flak	Crew	289

Carl Peters

Built by the Neptun yard in Rostock, *Carl Peters* was commissioned in January 1940 and became the depot ship for 1. S-Bootflottille. Her home base was in Kiel but operational deployment of her designated flotilla saw her based variously at Rotterdam and Ijmuiden in Holland, and at Abo in Finland. In April 1942 she took over 5. S-flottille and served with them in Norwegian waters, based first at Trondheim and then at Bodø. Remaining in Norway until December 1943, she returned to German waters to assist in the working-up of 21. S-flottille.

After a brief period of operational duty in early 1944 she returned to the training role, in which she remained until the end of the war. *Carl Peters* was sunk just a few days after the war when she ran onto uncleared mines.

U-bootsbegleitschiff *Weichsel* served as the depot ship for 3., 1., and then 22. U-Bootsflottillen. At the end of the war she was taken into service by the Royal Navy and renamed the *Royal Rupert*, before ultimately being handed over to the Soviet Union. (Deutsches U-Boot-Museum)

Specifications:			
Length	114m	Powerplant	4x MAN diesels
Beam	14.5m	Top speed	23 knots
Displacement	3,600 tons	Endurance	12,000 nautical miles
Armament	2x twin 10.5cm guns, 2x 8.8cm flak, 1x 4cm flak, 6x 3.7cm flak, 8x 2cm flak	Crew	225

Adolf Lüderitz

Sister ship to *Carl Peters*, the *Adolf Lüderitz* was commissioned in June 1940 and became the depot ship for 3. S-Bootflottille. She was based in Rotterdam until the opening of Operation 'Barbarossa' in mid 1941, when 3. S-flottille moved to the Baltic. In late 1941 she sailed for Norway to become depot ship for 8. S-flottille at Semskefjord and Kirkenes, and later for 6. S-flottille at Tromsø. Latterly, *Adolf Lüderitz* served as a wireless communications ship for U-boats operating out of Norway, before returning to Germany for a refit in February 1943. On completion of her refit she joined the S-Boot training flotilla and subsequently the S-Bootelehrdivision, where she remained until the end of the war. *Adolf Lüderitz* was allocated to the Soviet Union, and served as the *Paysherd*.

Specifications:			
Length	114m	Powerplant	4x MAN diesels
Beam	14.5m	Top speed	23 knots
Displacement	3,600 tons	Endurance	12,000 nautical miles
Armament	2x 10.5cm guns, 1x 4cm flak, 6x 3.7cm flak, 8x 2cm flak	Crew	225

Tsingtau

Built by Blohm & Voss in Hamburg, *Tsingtau* was launched in June 1934 and commissioned in September of that year. She was the first tender to be purpose-built as a support ship for the Schnellboote, but on the outbreak of war she actually served as a training ship for anti-aircraft crews. She eventually reverted to her intended role, and survived the war unscathed, going on to serve post-war with the GMSA under British control. She was eventually broken up in Great Britain in 1950.

Specifications:			
Length	87.5m	Powerplant	4x MAN diesels
Beam	13.5m	Top speed	17.5 knots
Displacement	2,400 tons	Endurance	8,500 nautical miles
Armament	2x 8.8cm guns, 8x 2cm flak	Crew	149

Tanga

Another product of the Neptun yard, this ship was built for export to China, but the Japanese invasion of that country prevented delivery. The vessel was taken over by the German Navy and commissioned as the *Tanga* in January 1939. She took over the 2. S-Bootflottille, operating in the Baltic until the beginning of 1940 and thereafter moving to Wilhelmshaven. Moving to the 6. S-flottille in March 1941, she remained with this training unit until moved to Norway in October 1941. She remained here for a year serving as a radio communications vessel for Kriegsmarine cruisers operating from Norway, returning to Germany in October 1942 for a refit. After its completion she joined the S-Bootlehrdivision, remaining as a depot ship for training units until January 1945; she then took over 11. S-flottille until the end of the war.

Painted in a striking disruptive camouflage pattern, this is either the U-boat depot ship *Wilhelm Bauer* or one of her sister ships *Waldermar Kophamel* or *Otto Wünsche*. The forward turret, just catching the sunlight, is a twin 10.5cm heavy flak mount. (Author's collection)

Thereafter the *Tanga* operated with the GMSA for two years, before being passed to the US Navy. She remained in American hands for a little over a year before transferring to the Danish Navy, with which she had a long and successful career until finally broken up in 1967.

Specifications:

Length	87.5m	Powerplant	4x MAN diesels
Beam	13.5m	Top speed	17 knots
Displacement	2,490 tons	Endurance	8,500 nautical miles
Armament	2x 8.8cm guns, 8x 2cm flak	Crew	149

Hela

Built by Stückelenwerft in Hamburg, *Hela* was launched in December 1938 and commissioned in October 1940. Designated as a Fleet Tender (Flottentender), she served throughout the war as a fleet command ship. Apart from minor damage suffered during an air raid in April 1945 she survived unscathed, and was taken over by the Soviets, serving as the *Angara*. Damage sustained during a fire in 1995 led to her being deactivated and serving as an accommodation ship. It appears that she has been refitted in more recent times and is up for sale – the sole remaining Kriegsmarine depot ship from World War II.

Specifications:

Length	100m	Powerplant	4x MAN diesels
Beam	12m	Top speed	21 knots
Displacement	2,520 tons	Endurance	2,000 nautical miles
Armament	2x 10.5cm guns, 2x 3.7cm flak, 2x 2cm flak	Crew	224

Saar

Built by Germaniawerft in Kiel and commissioned in October 1934, the *Saar* was the first purpose-built tender/support ship, and on being accepted into the Navy she took up her post as depot ship for 2. Unterseebootsflottille 'Saltzwedel'. During 1935 she served briefly as command ship for the U-boat training programme, before returning to her original role, at first with 1. U-flottille 'Weddigen' before returning in 1937 to 2. U-flottille. Following the outbreak of war the *Saar* took part in the invasion of Norway, serving as support ship to all of the U-boat units involved. By the end of the war she was serving as command ship for the Führer der Unterseeboote Ost, and after the end of hostilities she was handed over to the USA. In 1947 she passed to the French Navy, where she served as a workshop ship under the name *Gustave Zede*.

Specifications:

Length	100.5m	Powerplant	2x 4800hp diesels
Beam	13.5m	Top speed	18.3 knots
Displacement	3,250 tons	Endurance	7,265 nautical miles
Armament	3x 10.5cm flak, 8x 2cm flak	Crew	228

Schnellbootsbegleitschiff *Tanga*. Originally built for export to China, she was taken over by the Kriegsmarine first as an S-boat depot ship, and subsequently as a command ship for the Commanding Admiral for the North Sea. (Deutsches U-Boot-Museum)

ACCOMODATION SHIPS (Wohnschiffe)

The coming of war naturally freed up many German ships that had previously been used for leisure cruises, while the Navy found itself in need of accommodation for its sailors as the service expanded. The passenger ships had their bright civilian livery painted over with drab camouflage colours and were given a new career as accommodation ships, often for the crews of U-boat flotillas. Others were used as hospital ships. The two most important ships in this category were undoubtedly the ocean liners *Wilhelm Gustloff* and *Robert Ley*, which are often referred to as the world's first purpose-built cruise liners. Built for the Kraft durch Freude ('Strength through Joy') movement run by the Nazi DAF (German Labour Front – the Party organization that replaced free trade unions), these ships carried the movement's members on holiday cruises until 1939, when Germany's military needs saw both ships pressed into service with the Kriegsmarine.

Specifications for the class:			
Length	208.5m	Powerplant	6x 6-cylinder MAN diesels
Beam	23.6m	Top speed	15.5 knots
Displacement	25,484 tons	Endurance	12,000 nautical miles
Armament	3x 10.5cm flak, 8x 2cm flak		

Wilhelm Gustloff

Built by Blohm & Voss in Hamburg, and launched in May 1927, the *Wilhelm Gustloff* first served in a military role at the end of May 1939 when she transported members of the Condor Legion, who had been serving in the Spanish Civil War, from Vigo back to Hamburg. On the outbreak of war she was for some time pressed into service as a hospital ship. Latterly, the *Gustloff* was employed as an accommodation ship for men of the 2. Unterseeboots-Lehrdivision in Gotenhafen. As the Red Army approached East Prussia in January 1945, it was decided that she would be one of the vessels used to evacuate a mixture of Kriegsmarine personnel, wounded soldiers and civilian refugees from the Samland peninsula north of Königsberg west down the Baltic to safety at Kiel. Her normal capacity was 1,465 passengers; although exact numbers can never be known, it is thought that when she departed on 30 January 1945 she was crammed with around 10,580, of whom about 8,950 were civilians.

Escorted by the torpedo boat *Möwe*, the *Wilhelm Gustloff* was running with her navigation lights illuminated, trying to avoid a collision with a minesweeper flotilla thought to be operating in the vicinity. Just east of Leba the lights attracted the attention of the Soviet submarine S-13, which fired three torpedoes; all of them hit the liner, which sank within 45 minutes. The most recent estimates suggest that despite the rescue efforts of naval vessels that rushed to the site, around 9,400 souls were lost in the freezing Baltic waters that night, making the *Gustloff* tragedy the worst single sea disaster in recorded history.

Robert Ley

Launched in March 1938, the *Robert Ley* had a wartime career very similar to that of her sister ship. She was used to bring members of the Condor Legion back to Germany in May 1939, and on the outbreak of hostilities was converted for use as a hospital ship. Subsequently she served as an accommodation ship at Neustadt, with 1. Unterseeboots- Lehrdivision and 21. U-flottille. In the closing stages of the war *Robert Ley* was also used for the evacuation of wounded soldiers and civilian refugees from the Baltic coast. She was seriously damaged during a bombing raid while berthed in Hamburg on 9 March 1945. After the war she was taken to Britain and scrapped.

MISCELLANEOUS VESSELS

The Kriegsmarine naturally had large numbers of miscellaneous vessels, many of which were built in very small numbers or were even 'one-off' types for special purposes. They included the following:

1: Schnellbootsbegleitschiff *Carl Peters*

This class of flotilla depot/escort ships was visually very similar to the *Wilhelm Bauer* class of U-Bootbegleitschiffe, but was about 20m shorter and around 2,000 tons lighter in displacement. In keeping with its largely static role its armament consists of anti-aircraft guns, the main weapons being two twin 10.5cm flak turrets. These replaced the lighter twin 8.8cm flak turrets originally installed, and were in turn replaced by two single 10.5cm turrets in 1944.

2: Sperrbrecher

The large number of different types of vessel were utilized in the role of 'barrier-breaker', leading Kriegsmarine warships in and out of port through minefield lanes. The example shown here is *Sperrbrecher 1*, which began life as the freighter *Saar*, built in 1935 by Deschimag in Bremen. She displaced 3,200 tons and was powered by two MAN 6-cylinder diesels, which gave her a speed of around 14 knots. She was armed with 2x 10.5cm, 6x 3.7cm and up to 12x 2cm guns. Like many Sperrbrecher she also carried her own barrage balloon. She was eventually scuttled in the docks at Brest in August 1944.

3: Tross-schiff (*Dithmarschen* class)

This is a typical example of the *Dithmarschen* class naval supply ship; all vessels within the class were built to near-identical specifications. Armament consisted of 3x 15cm guns which had previously been mounted on old torpedo boats. Since these ships had originally been designed with the capability of serving as auxiliary cruisers – commerce raiders – one gun was concealed behind folding panels at the side of the bridge, and another inside a false deckhouse at the stern. In addition 2x 3.7cm and between 4x and 8x 2cm flak guns were carried. Unlike many other auxiliary supply ships the *Dithmarschen* class was specifically built for naval rather than civil use.

4: Lazarettschiff *Robert Ley*

Named after the head of the Nazi DAF (Deutsches Arbeits Front), she and her ill-fated sister ship *Wilhelm Gustloff* were built as cruise liners for the Kraft durch Freude ('Strength through Joy') movement, which gave working-class Germans the chance to enjoy the type of holiday until then the preserve of the wealthy. She is shown here in her guise as a hospital ship in late 1939.

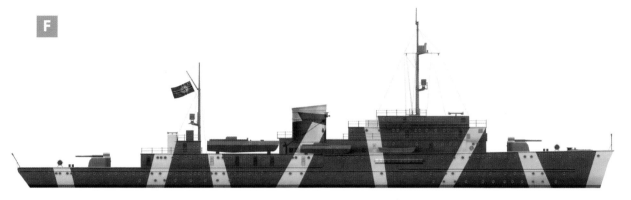

1: Schnellbootsbegleitschiff *Carl Peters*

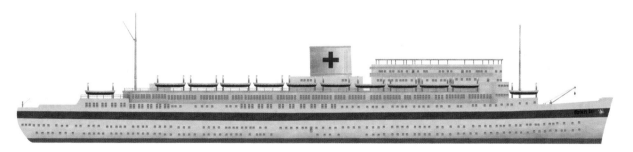

2: Sperrbrecher

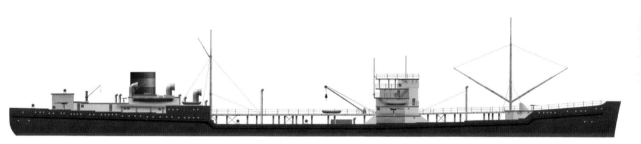

3: Tross-schiff (*Dithmarschen* class)

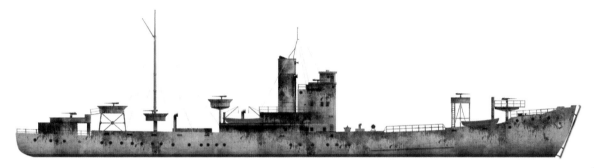

4: Lazarettschiff *Robert Ley*

State yacht

Built by Blohm & Voss and commissioned in May 1935, *Aviso Grille* was Germany's state yacht. She was used on a number of occasions by Hitler to host visiting foreign dignitaries during naval reviews and other formal occasions, as well as making several goodwill visits to various countries including Great Britain. *Grille* was used as a test-bed for the high-pressure steam turbines being produced for the Navy's new destroyers. On the outbreak of war she reverted to an operational military role, and was used to lay mines off the French coast. She was later transferred to the Baltic, and from her base at Swinemünde she carried out predominantly patrol work. Thereafter she was used for gunnery training duties until the invasion of the Soviet Union in June 1941 when she once again took up minelaying duties, this time in the Baltic, before returning to gunnery training. After a refit in 1942 she sailed for Norwegian waters, where she remained as a base ship for the remainder of the war. *Grille* passed into British hands at the end of the war and was subsequently sold off into civilian ownership. She was eventually scrapped in the USA in 1951.

TOP
U-Bootsbegleitschiff *Saar*, the first of the U-boat depot ships, was originally classed as a fleet tender before being allocated to the first operational flotilla of Germany's new U-boat arm. (Deutsches U-Boot-Museum)

BELOW
The ocean liner *Robert Ley*, shown here pre-war as a cruise ship with the 'Strength through Joy' movement, ended up as an accommodation ship with the Kriegsmarine. Her sister ship *Wilhelm Gustloff* was sunk in the Baltic in January 1945 with the greatest loss of life ever recorded in a single maritime disaster. (Deutsches U-Boot-Museum)

Specifications:				
Length	135m	Powerplant	2x Blohm & Voss steam turbines
Beam	13.5m	Top speed	26 knots
Displacement	3,430 tons	Endurance	9,500 nautical miles
Armament	2x 10.5cm guns, 2x 3.7cm flak, 2x 2cm flak; up to 228 mines	Crew	250

Versuchsboote

Literally 'test boats', these were generally old ships, usually veterans of World War I which were too outdated for operational use and were simply retained as test-beds for new equipment or methods. Some did see occasional active service, however, being used as support vessels during the invasions of Norway and Denmark. A few of the newer boats did see service throughout the war; for example, Versuchsboot *Pelikan*, a former mine warfare test boat of the Kaiserliche Marine, served on convoy escort duties in the Kattegat throughout the war, and was considered worth being taken over by the Americans in 1945.

Some of these vessels, like *Pelikan* and *Claus von Bevern*, had been built as warships; others had civilian origins – like the Welle, built as a fishing boat. These boats were simply classed together by purpose rather than by design or type. Thirteen vessels were so designated, as follows: Versuchsboot *Acheron*, Versuchsboot *Arkona*, Versuchsboot *Claus von Bevern*, Versuchsboot *Grille*, Versuchsboot *Hecht*, Versuchsboot *Johann Wittenborg*, Versuchsboot *Nautilus*, Versuchsboot *Otto Braun*, Versuchsboot *Pelikan*, Versuchsboot *Störtebecker*, Versuchsboot *Strahl*, Versuchsboot *Sundewall* and Versuchsboot *Welle*.

Schulschiffe

In addition to existing older ships inhertited from the Kaiserliche Marine and Reichsmarine, two newly built vessels were designated as school ships – the *Brummer* and *Bremse*.

Brummer was launched in May 1935 at Deschimag in Bremen and commissioned in February 1936. As well as her intended duties in training anti-aircraft crews, it was planned that when necessary she could act as an auxiliary minelayer, and in that capacity she could carry up to 450 mines. *Brummer's* main armament consisted of twin 10.5cm heavy flak mounts of the same type as used on most of Germany's heavy warships. It is interesting to note that she was used as a test-bed for the new high-pressure steam turbines that would be fitted into Germany's destroyer fleet, and that on *Brummer* they were found to work well, in contrast to their highly problematic performance on the destroyers.

Serving initially at the Küstenartillerieschule at Swinemünde, on the outbreak of war *Brummer* transferred to minelaying duties and in April 1940 was allocated to the invasion forces being assembled for the invasion of Norway and Denmark. On 14 April she was hit by torpedoes from the British submarine HMS *Starlet*, and the resultant explosion blew off almost her entire foredeck. Despite several hours of desperate attempts to save her, she rolled over and sank early on 15 April.

Specifications:				
Length	113m	Powerplant	2x 8,000hp high-pressure steam turbines
Beam	13.5m	Top speed	23 knots
Displacement	3,010 tons	Endurance	2,400 nautical miles
Armament	8x 10.5cm flak, 2x 8.8 cm flak, 8x 3.7cm flak, 4x 2cm flak	Crew	238 (including trainees)

Considerably smaller than *Brummer*, the *Bremse* was launched in January 1931 at the Kriegsmarine Werft in Wilhelmshaven and commissioned into the Navy in July 1932. Until 1939 Bremse served in her intended role as a training ship for naval anti-aircraft crews. On the outbreak of war she was allocated to escort duties for minelaying and troop ships in the Baltic before returning briefly to training duties.

In April 1940, however, like *Brummer*, she was allocated to the invasion forces for Unternehmen Weserübung. During the invasion of Norway she

The *Aviso Grille* was Germany's state yacht, often used to host foreign dignitaries at naval events pre-war. During wartime her duties included acting as an auxiliary minelayer. (Deutsches U-Boot-Museum)

The Artillerieschuleschiff *Bremse*, the smaller of Germany's two purpose-built gunnery training ships. Used as an escort ship during the war, she was sunk in a gun battle with British cruisers in September 1941 while escorting a convoy in the North Sea. (Deutsches U-Boot-Museum)

suffered three direct hits from heavy shore batteries, but was able to land the troops she was carrying and continue, sinking some minor Norwegian naval vessels before running aground. She was forced into Stavanger for repairs and was out of action for three months before she could return to Germany.

Bremse was operating in the North Sea when, on 30 July 1941, she came under heavy attack by Fairey Albacore torpedo-bombers and Fairey Fulmar fighters from the British carrier HMS *Victorious*, but escaped any serious damage. In early September 1941, operating from a base in Norway, *Bremse*, together with an armed trawler and a torpedo boat, was escorting a convoy heading towards the Murmansk front when, on the night of 8 September, the convoy was intercepted by a British naval force consisting of the cruisers HMS *Aurora* and *Nigeria* supported by destroyers. The German warships engaged, but in the nocturnal artillery duel that followed all three of them were sunk; *Bremse* took 160 of her crew down with her. The sacrifice of the three small warships allowed the convoy to escape unscathed.

Specifications:			
Length	103.5m	Powerplant	2x 8-cylinder 28,000hp MAN diesels
Beam	9.5m	Top speed	29 knots
Displacement	1,870 tons	Endurance	8,000 nautical miles
Armament	4x 12.7cm guns, 4x 3.7cm flak, 8x 2cm flak	Crew	290 (including trainees)

Apart from these two purpose-built Artillerieschulschiffe, the following older vessels were also classed as Schulboote: Artillerieschuleboot *Hay*, Artillerieschulboot *Fuchs*, Artillerieschulboot *Jungmann* and Artillerieschulboot *Delphin*.

G **SEGELSCHULSCHIFF *HORST WESSEL*, LATE 1930s**

Probably the most aesthetically pleasing of all of the Kriegsmarine's vessels were the Segelschulschiffe. Three almost identical sister ships were built between 1933 and 1937: the *Horst Wessel*, *Gorch Fock* and *Albert Leo Schlageter*. Around 90m in length and displacing between 1,550 and 1,750 tons, these steel-hulled, three-masted barques were intended to give officer and petty officer candidates of the German Navy a taste of life 'before the mast' and an opportunity to learn the traditional skills of seamanship. Although many of these might not have been applicable to service on modern warships, the character-building element of these training cruises was undeniable. These ships did carry armament for training purposes, consisting of a small number of 2cm flak guns. At the outbreak of war they were relegated to more mundane tasks such as floating administrative offices or transport vessels. It is a testament to the soundness of their design and construction that all three are still in existence today, and two are still in seagoing service – albeit not in the service of their nation of origin.

This plate shows *Horst Wessel* in her glory days, running under full sail across the Atlantic on a pre-war training cruise to the Caribbean. The diesel auxiliary motor would be used to manoeuvre the ship in and out of port and for periods of total calm. Otherwise, the full power of the wind in her almost 2,000 square metres of sail would be more than sufficient to propel her across the waves. Note the large eagle-and-swastika figurehead; this was removed on the outbreak of war. Ironically, she still bears a similar figurehead today (though without the swastika) in her current guise as the US Coast Guard cutter *Eagle*.

Vermessungsschiff Meteor

There was also a diver training boat, Taucherschulboot *Taucher*, and two designated simply as school boats – Schulboot *Spree* and Schulboot *Freyr*. Schulboot *Spree* was for a time the home of the so-called Unterseebootsabwehrschule which, despite being named as an anti-submarine warfare school, was actually an establishment for secretly training new U-boat crews before Germany began openly re-arming. Both *Spree* and *Freyr* were former fishing vessels taken over by the military.

Fischereischutzboote

Three Kriegsmarine vessels were designated for fishery protection duties, these being Fischereischutzboot *Zieten*, and the sister ships Fischereischutzboot *Elbe* and Fischereischutzboot *Weser*. Both *Elbe* and *Weser* were built in 1931 and served in the fishery protection service until 1938, at which point they and *Zieten* were refitted as tenders for R-boats. They saw service in the English Channel, the Baltic and in Norway. After the war they served with the GMSA, operating out of Cuxhaven; *Elbe* was handed over to the USSR in December 1945.

Vermessungsschiffe

Two vessels were designated as oceanic research ships, Vermessungsschiff *Meteor* and Vermessungsschiff *Panther*. Both were veterans of World War I, originally built as gunboats for the Kaiser's navy. The Kriegsmarine made use of such boats before the outbreak of war (the *Meteor* completed research trips to study the Gulf Stream and the waters of the far North Atlantic), but by September 1939 both had been decommissioned. *Meteor* was brought back into service in 1940 and remained in use as a research ship, based first in Denmark and then in Norway; she ended the war back in Germany, where she was handed over to the USSR.

SAIL TRAINING SHIPS (Segelschulschiffe)

Germany's sail training programme for officers and cadets suffered a tragedy when in 1932 the sailing ship *Niobe* capsized in a storm with considerable loss of life. A programme of construction resulted in the appearance in the late 1930s of three new sister ships of a new class of three-masted barques: the *Albert Leo Schlageter*, the *Horst Wessel* and the *Gorch Fock*. These beautiful ships were to be responsible for training a new generation of naval officer cadets in seamanship over the next few years, carrying out goodwill cruises to a number of foreign ports throughout the world.

Albert Leo Schlageter

After the outbreak of war brought her sail training voyages to an end, *Albert Leo Schlageter* remained in port where she served as an administration ship – in effect, floating offices. However, she was recalled to service in the Baltic in 1944, and in November of that year ran onto a Soviet mine and had to be towed back to port. She was in Flensburg at the end of the war, and was handed over to the US Navy, who retained her for three years before selling her to Brazil. She remained there until 1961, when she was sold on to Portugal, and is still in service to this day as the *Sagres*.

Horst Wessel

On the outbreak of war *Horst Wessel's* training duties were severely curtailed though not completely stopped, and she began a new role as a military transport ship; during operations in the Baltic she was even credited with shooting down three Soviet aircraft. After repairs and refitting in Wilhelmshaven at the end of the war, *Horst Wessel* was handed over to the US Navy, and in 1946 she was commissioned into the US Coastguard as the Coastguard Cutter *Eagle*; she is still in service today.

Gorch Fock

On the outbreak of war *Gorch Fock,* like her sister ship *Albert Leo Schlageter,* was used as a floating administrative office, based in Stralsund. She was formally reactivated in April 1944; and in May 1945, as Soviet forces approached, she was taken into shallow waters near Rügen and scuttled. However, she was raised by the Soviets and completely repaired and refitted; she served her new masters as the *Tovarisch*, taking part in many international 'Tall Ships' races. On the break-up of the Soviet Union she found herself under Ukrainian ownership. In 1995 she was sold and taken to Great Britain for a complete refit; from there she was sold once again, to German owners, returning to her country of origin and being renamed *Gorch Fock*. She is currently a museum ship.

It is interesting to note that Germany commissioned a new *Gorch Fock* in 1958, built to the same plans as the original with only a few modifications to bring her up to modern safety specifications.

All of the class carried around 2,000m² of sail as well as the diesel auxiliary engine, and were fitted with a small number of 2cm flak guns for weapons training.

The Segelschulschiff Gorch Fock, one of three beautiful three-masted barques built to give prospective naval officers a taste of life 'before the mast'. This fine vessel survived the war and is still in existence today. (Deutsches U-Boot-Museum)

Specifications for the class:			
Length	89m	Top speed	17 knots
Beam	12m	Endurance	8,000 nautical miles
Displacement	1,755 tons	Crew	Up to 290 (including trainees)
Powerplant	750hp diesel auxiliary engine		

INDEX

Figures in **bold** refer to illustrations. Plates are shown with page and caption locators in brackets.